Bulk discounts available for educational purposes, reselling, gifts, or fundraising campaigns.
Email: author@thegoldenquest.com

Publisher's Cataloging-In-Publication Data
(Prepared by The Donohue Group, Inc.)

Names: Delisle, David, author. | Hanson, Travis, illustrator.
Title: The golden quest : your journey to a rich life / by David Delisle ;
          [illustrated by Travis Hanson].
Description: First edition. | [Victoria, British Columbia] : David Delisle, 2021. | Interest age level: 5 and up. | Summary: "... an
          illustrated adventure about a young boy who embarks on a Hero's Journey
          with his dog Shelby to discover the Golden Rules of Money"--Provided by
          publisher.
Identifiers: ISBN 9781777718909 (hardback) | ISBN 9781777718916 (ebook) | ISBN 978177718923 (softcover)
Subjects: LCSH: Boys--Juvenile fiction. | Money--Juvenile fiction. | Dogs-
          -Juvenile fiction. | Adventure and adventurers--Juvenile fiction. |
          CYAC: Boys--Fiction. | Money--Fiction. | Dogs--Fiction. |
          Adventure and adventurers--Fiction.
Classification: LCC PZ7.1.D4557 Go 2021 (print) | LCC PZ7.1.D4557 (ebook)
          | DDC [E]--dc23

the Golden Quest
Your Journey to a Richer Life

David Delisle

Dedicated to my boys, Will & Noah.

You were the inspiration to begin this journey and I wanted to thank you for all of your help, laughter and joy every step of the way. There is nothing that I'm more proud of than being your Dad.

You are my Awesome Stuff.

THE Journey Begins

"A journey of a thousand miles begins
with a single step."
– Lao Tzu

2

4

5

7

GOOD LUCK AND BE SAFE, AND REMEMBER TO WEAR YOUR COAT, AND DON'T FORGET TO BRUSH, AND...

DON'T WORRY, MOM, I'LL BE FINE.

THE Awesome Stuff

"Wealth consists not in having great possessions, but in having few wants."
– Epictetus

THUNK!

THUNK!

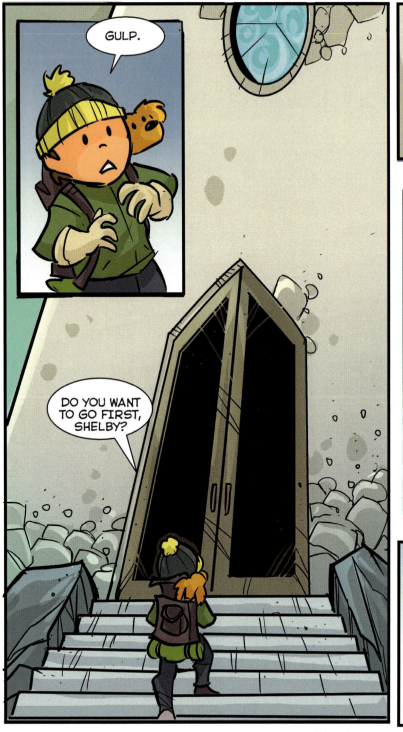

14

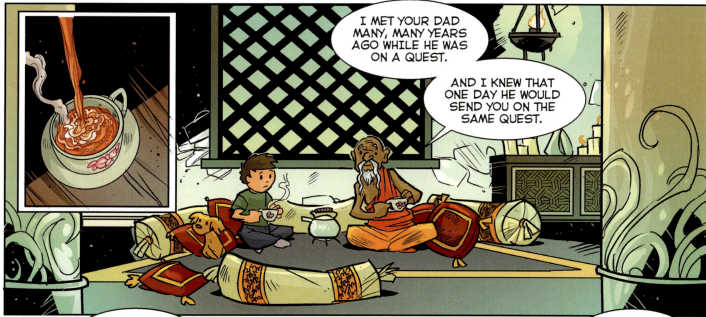

17

19

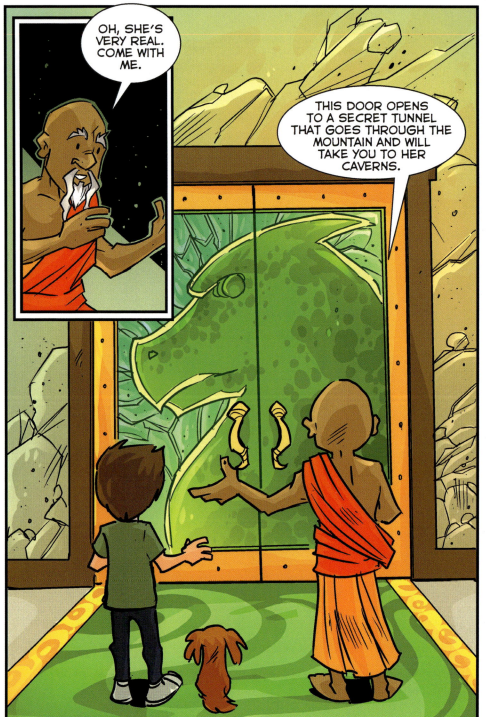

20

23

25

28

29

34

WOOF WOOF!

HI! I'M HERE FOR THE JOB YOU POSTED.

40

DID THE DRAGON OF THE CRYSTAL CAVERNS SEND YOU?

EXCELLENT. FOR TODAY'S LESSON, I'LL TEACH YOU HOW TO GROW YOUR SAVINGS EVEN MORE...

YES. SHE TAUGHT ME TO "ALWAYS SAVE FIRST" IF I WANT MY SAVINGS TO GROW.

...BY NOT LETTING YOUR SAVINGS SIT AROUND DOING NOTHING.

INSTEAD, INVEST YOUR SAVINGS.

INVEST? WHAT IS THAT?

IT'S LIKE SENDING YOUR SAVINGS TO WORK.

43

IF $500 DOUBLES ONCE, IT WILL GROW TO $1000.

IF IT DOUBLES 10 TIMES, IT WILL GROW TO $500,000.

AND IF YOU STARTED 7 YEARS EARLIER AND IT DOUBLED JUST ONE MORE TIME IT WILL GROW TO... $1,000,000.

46

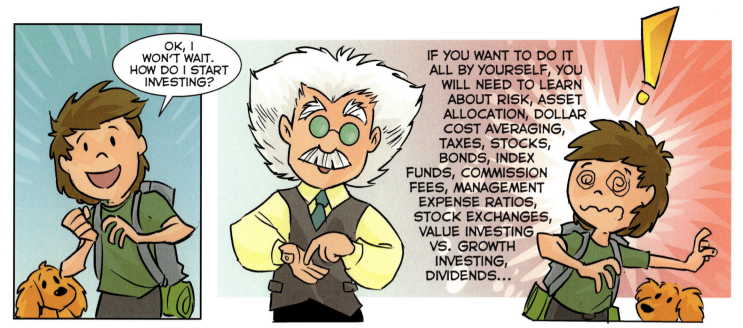

48

49

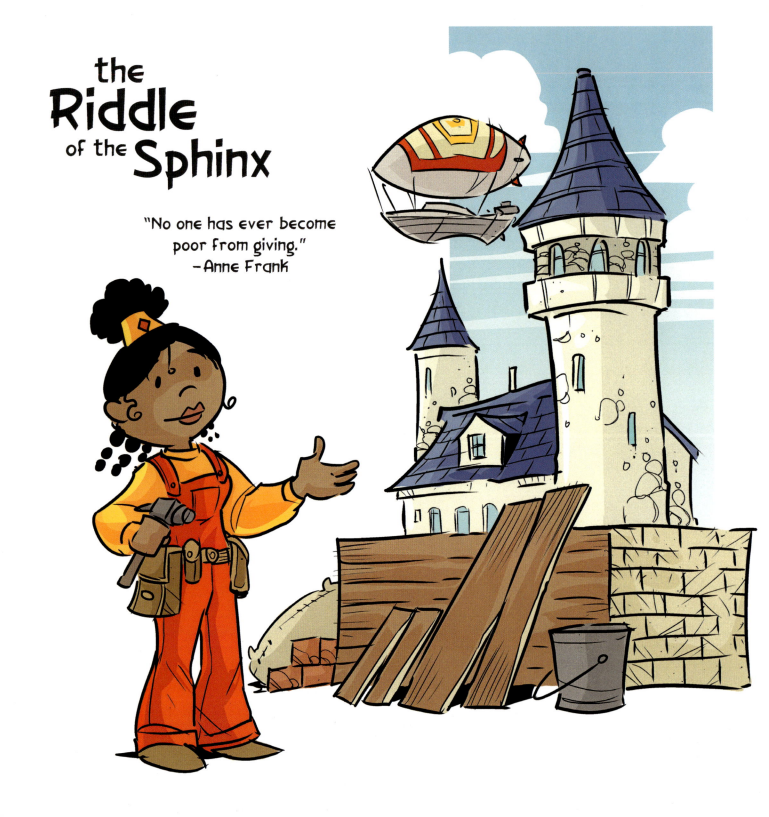

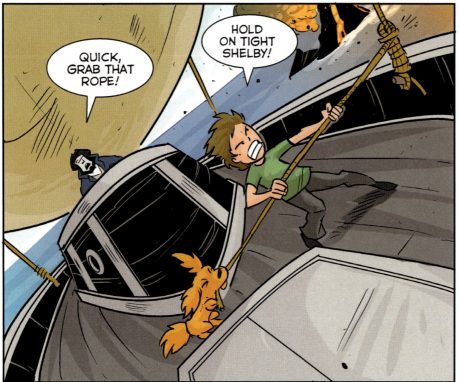

52

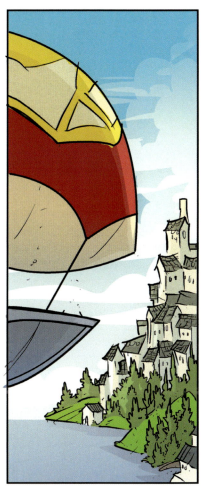

HERE WE ARE. SAFE AND SOUND JUST LIKE I PROMISED.

THANKS.

I'LL JUST WAIT HERE.

RACE YOU THERE, SHELBY!

WOOF WOOF!

58

...SHE CAME ACROSS A FARMER PLOWING HIS FIELD WITH AN OLD HAND PUSH PLOW.

HE LOOKED LIKE HE COULD USE SOME HELP.

SO SHE GAVE HIM SOME OF HER GOLD.

WITH THE GOLD, HE BOUGHT A HORSE AND A NEW PLOW.

HE WAS ABLE TO PLOW MORE...

...AND HARVEST MORE.

AND SOMETHING AMAZING HAPPENED.

BEING ABLE TO HELP THE FARMER MADE THE YOUNG BLACKSMITH REALIZE HOW MUCH SHE ALREADY HAD.

62

HER WORKSHOP GREW.

SO, SHE GAVE MORE.

THE MORE SHE GAVE AND HELPED HER NEIGHBORS, THE MORE THEY HELPED HER.

AND HER WORKSHOP GREW EVEN MORE.

THE MORE SHE GAVE, THE RICHER SHE BECAME.

THE SPHINX WAS RIGHT! SHE WAS RICH.

YES, AND NOT JUST IN GOLD.

SHE WAS RICH IN MORE WAYS THAN SHE HAD EVER IMAGINED.

BUT WHAT WAS EVEN MORE AMAZING WAS THAT THE MORE SHE GAVE...

...THE MORE IT INSPIRED OTHERS TO GIVE.

67

the Final Lesson

"Time is the most valuable thing
a (person) can spend."
–Theophrastus

73

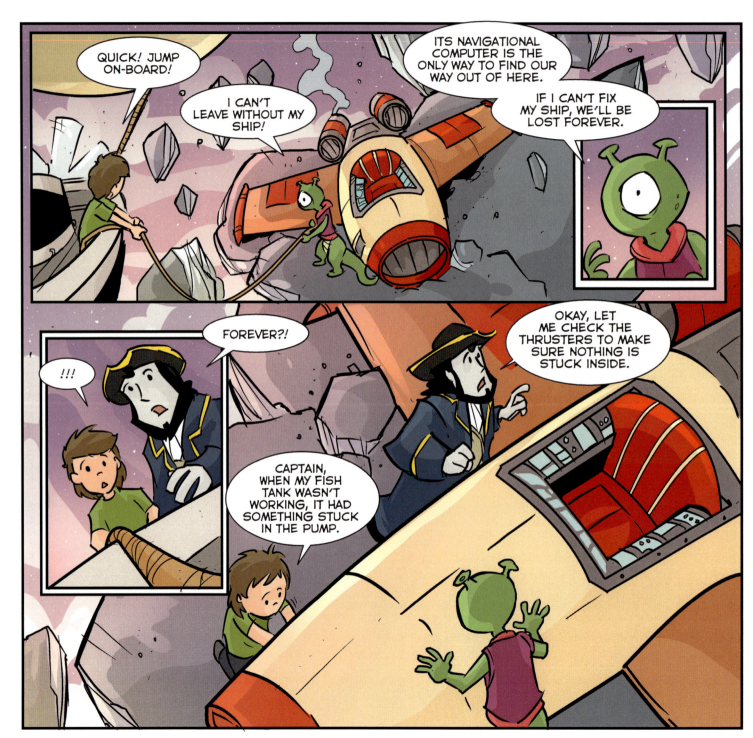

74

75

77

79

BUT IF HAPPINESS DOESN'T COME FROM HAVING MORE...

...WHY SHOULD I FOLLOW THE GOLDEN RULES OF MONEY AND SAVE SO MUCH?

82

83

84

85

27 YEARS LATER.

HAPPY BIRTH

THE GOLDEN RULES

Golden Rule #1: Only buy the awesome stuff.

Golden Rule #2: Always save first.

Golden Rule #3: Send your savings to work TO-DAY.

Golden Rule #4: Give and you'll have more.

Follow the Golden Rules of Money so you'll have more freedom for what's most important to YOU. The Awesome Stuff.

Thank you so much for being a part of this journey.

If you know someone who would benefit from reading The Golden Quest, please consider sharing this story with them.

The author is also available for speaking engagements to teach both parents and kids important lessons about money.

Bulk discounts are available for orders of 10 copies or more.

Please contact the author for more details.
Email: author@thegoldenquest.com

Join The Awesome Stuff newsletter for exclusive insights and claim your free step-by-step guide on talking with your kids about money.

The Awesome Stuff™
www.theawesomestuff.com

Printed in Japan
落丁、乱丁本のお問い合わせは
Amazon.co.jp カスタマーサービスへ

12845898R00059